Plant Top Tens

Australasia's Most Amazing Plants

Raintree

www.raintreepublishers.co.uk
Visit our website to find out more information about Raintree Books.

To order:
☎ Phone 44 (0) 1865 888112
▤ Send a fax to 44 (0) 1865 314091
▢ Visit the Raintree Bookshop at **www.raintreepublishers.co.uk** to browse our catalogue and order online

Raintree is an imprint of Capstone Global Library Limited, a company incorporated in England and Wales having its registered office at 7 Pilgrim Street, London, EC4V 6LB – Registered company number: 6695582

"Raintree" is a registered trademark of Pearson Education Limited, under licence to Capstone Global Library Limited

Produced for Raintree by Calcium

Editorial: Kate de Villiers and Sarah Eason
Design: Victoria Bevan and Paul Myerscough
Illustrations: Geoff Ward
Picture Research: Maria Joannou
Originated by Modern Age
Printed and bound by China Translation Printing Services

ISBN 978 1 4062 0969 3 (hardback)
12 11 10 09 08
10 9 8 7 6 5 4 3 2 1

ISBN 978 1 4062 0976 1 (paperback)
13 12 11 10 09
10 9 8 7 6 5 4 3 2 1

British Library Cataloguing in Publication Data
Scott, Michael and Royston, Angela
   Australasia. - (Plant top tens)
   581.9'9
A full catalogue record for this book is available from the British Library.

Acknowledgements
The authors and publisher are grateful to the following for permission to reproduce copyright material: © Alamy Images pp. 20 (AA World Travel Library), 21 (Craig Lovell/Eagle Visions Photography), 27 (Mark Nemeth); © Corbis p. 19 (Jonathan Marks); © Dreamstime p. 13 (Irina Yun); © FLPA p. 25 (Fred Bavendam/Minden Pictures); © Getty Images p. 9; © iStockphoto p. 17; © Nature Picture Library p. 4 (Tony Heald); © NHPA pp. 7 (Daniel Zupanc), 24 (Pete Atkinson); © PA Photos p. 22 (AP Photo/Royal Botanic Gardens, Jaime Plaza); © Photolibrary pp. 8, 12 (Photolibrary/Dani/Jeske), 16 (Robin Smith), 23 (Rick Price); © Rex Features p. 15 (Wildtrack Media); © Kris Schaffer p. 26 (courtesy Peter Lawson); © Science Photo Library p. 11 (Fletcher & Baylis); © Shutterstock pp. 6, 10, 14, 18 (Michael Fuery).

Cover photograph of a banksia reproduced with permission of FLPA/Frans Lanting.

Every effort has been made to contact copyright holders of any material reproduced in this book. Any omissions will be rectified in subsequent printings if notice is given to the publishers.

Contents

Some words are printed in bold, **like this**. You can find out what they mean on page 31 in the Glossary.

Australasia

Australasia includes Australia and New Zealand, as well as Fiji and other smaller islands north-east of Australia. Australasia has many different types of **habitat**. A habitat includes the landscape and all the plants and animals that live there.

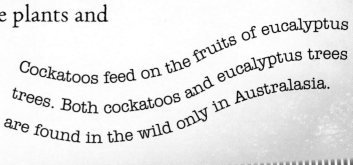

Cockatoos feed on the fruits of eucalyptus trees. Both cockatoos and eucalyptus trees are found in the wild only in Australasia.

Separate worlds

Most of the types of plant that grow in Australasia do not grow in the wild anywhere else in the world. This is because Australia and New Zealand have been separated from the rest of the world for millions of years. The plants growing here gradually became different.

0   500 miles
0   500 kilometres

N
W — E
S

Papua
New
Guinea

Indian Ocean

Great
Barrier
Reef

Great
Sandy Desert

AUSTRALIA

Simpson Desert

Great Victoria Desert   Lake Eyre

Key
- rainforest
- desert
- grassland
- mountains
- coral reef
- borderlines

Pacific Ocean

North
Island

**NEW
ZEALAND**

Southern Ocean

Tasmania

Southern Alps

South Island

Australasia

Australasia's habitat

Most of Australia is **desert** and dry **grassland**, except around the coast. The desert is too dry for many plants to grow, and few types of plant grow on the grassland. Australia and New Zealand have high mountains. Only a few plants can grow here. But Australasia also has **tropical rainforests** and woodlands. The Pacific islands are mostly tropical forest.

Gum tree

There are many kinds of gum tree. The giant gum is the tallest **broad-leaved** tree in the world. Other kinds of gum tree grow no bigger than bushes. Gum trees grow well in many different habitats. Some grow in the desert and others grow at the top of mountains. All of them grow very fast.

Koalas eat only gum tree leaves.

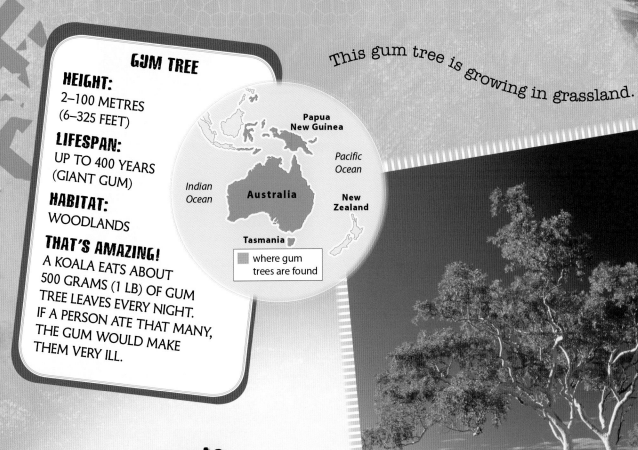

GUM TREE

HEIGHT:
2–100 METRES
(6–325 FEET)

LIFESPAN:
UP TO 400 YEARS
(GIANT GUM)

HABITAT:
WOODLANDS

THAT'S AMAZING!
A KOALA EATS ABOUT
500 GRAMS (1 LB) OF GUM
TREE LEAVES EVERY NIGHT.
IF A PERSON ATE THAT MANY,
THE GUM WOULD MAKE
THEM VERY ILL.

Papua
New Guinea

Pacific
Ocean

Indian
Ocean

Australia

New
Zealand

Tasmania

where gum
trees are found

Tough roots

Gum trees often grow
where **wildfires** are
common. The wood and
leaves contain an oil, or
"gum", that burns very
easily. The gum makes the
tree burn quickly, but the
roots are so tough they survive. When the fire
has passed, the roots put up new shoots. So
many of these grow, and so fast, that they crowd
out all the other plants!

strangler fig

A strangler fig grows in the **rainforest**. It grows around the trunk of another tree and then kills it! Rainforest trees grow so close together that they struggle to get enough sunlight. The strangler fig solves the problem by starting to grow halfway up a tall tree. The **seed** grows in soil made by rotted leaves trapped between the branches of the tree.

This strangler fig is hollow in the middle because the fig has killed the tree it originally grew on.

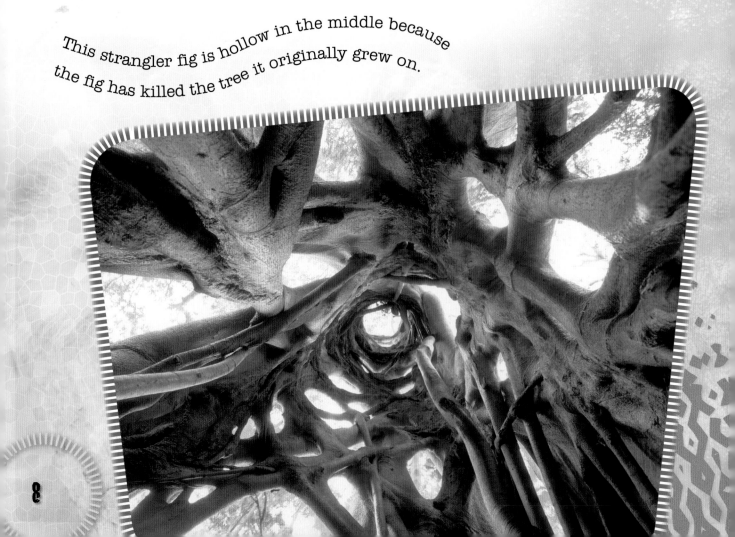

Strangler figs cover trees with their roots.

Tree killer

The strangler fig's roots grow around the tree and down to the ground. There they take in more **nutrients**, and the fig grows even stronger. Its branches and leaves cover every part of the tree and stop it getting sunlight. The original tree slowly dies. Then the huge strangler fig stands on its own. In the centre of it is a large hollow where the original tree used to be!

STRANGLER FIG

HEIGHT:
UP TO 60 METRES (195 FEET)

LIFESPAN:
SEVERAL HUNDRED YEARS

HABITAT:
RAINFOREST

THAT'S AMAZING!
WHEN BIRDS AND SMALL ANIMALS EAT THE FRUIT OF STRANGLER FIGS, THE SEEDS PASS THROUGH THEIR BODIES. SOME DROP INTO SOIL HIGH IN THE TREES AND BEGIN TO GROW THERE.

Papua New Guinea

Pacific Ocean

Indian Ocean

Australia

New Zealand

Tasmania

where strangler figs are found

Maiden veil toadstool

Maiden veil toadstools grow in rainforests. Each toadstool has a brown cap that is covered with tiny seeds called **spores**. The toadstool smells like rotting meat! The stink attracts flies. As the flies crawl through the lacy veil, spores spill from the cap on to their backs. The spores later fall to the ground and start to grow in another part of the forest.

MAIDEN VEIL TOADSTOOL

HEIGHT:
UP TO 20 CENTIMETRES (8 INCHES)

LIFESPAN:
THE TOADSTOOL LASTS ONLY A FEW DAYS

HABITAT:
RAINFOREST

THAT'S AMAZING!
MAIDEN VEIL TOADSTOOLS SMELL SO BAD, PEOPLE CANNOT BEAR THE SMELL EVEN 90 METRES (300 FEET) AWAY.

Papua New Guinea

Pacific Ocean

Indian Ocean

Australia

New Zealand

Tasmania

where maiden veil toadstools are found

A maiden veil toadstool has a white lacy veil that hangs down from the cap.

Not a true plant

Toadstools are **fungi**. They are not true plants because they do not make their own food. Instead they feed on the nutrients in dead leaves. They help to break down the leaves so that the rest of their nutrients go back into the soil, to feed other plants.

Maiden veil toadstools and other fungi help to break down fallen leaves.

Toadstools
A toadstool or mushroom is the part of a fungus that produces spores. The rest of the fungus consists of tiny threads that creep through the soil.

Mamaku

A mamaku is a fern that grows as tall as a tree! Most ferns grow in shady, wet places, because they lose water easily. However, the mamaku is good at taking in water and so it grows in sunny woods. It has special roots that cover its trunk. They take in water from the air when it is damp, and from rain that runs down the trunk.

Mamakus are tree-ferns. They are not real trees because their **stems** are not made of wood.

Roots

The roots of plants take in water and nutrients. Roots that grow in the soil also anchor the plant in the ground.

Super leaves

Ferns have long leaves called **fronds**. The fronds of the mamaku can be 5 metres (16 feet) long. Only two or three new fronds grow each year. They are rolled up tight and then uncurl like a party whistle that straightens when you blow into it.

MAMAKU

HEIGHT:
UP TO 20 METRES (65 FEET)

LIFESPAN:
50–100 YEARS

HABITAT:
OPEN WOODLAND

THAT'S AMAZING!
TREE-FERNS HAVE BEEN ON EARTH LONGER THAN MOST OTHER PLANTS. DINOSAURS USED TO ROAM THROUGH FORESTS OF TREE-FERNS.

Papua New Guinea

Pacific Ocean

Indian Ocean

Australia

New Zealand

Tasmania

where mamakus are found

This new leaf is ready to uncurl.

Banksia

The **flower head** of a banksia contains about a thousand tiny flowers! Most flowers have **pollen** at their centre, but banksias have pollen around the outside of the flower head. This helps the pollen to stick to birds and insects. They carry the pollen to other flowers so that these flowers can make seeds.

The flower head of a banksia looks like a brush for cleaning bottles.

Pollen

Male pollen from one flower joins with the female eggs of another flower. The eggs then become seeds that can grow into new plants.

This honey possum carries pollen from one flower to another.

Woody cone

After the seeds of a banksia have formed, a woody **cone** grows around them. Usually the cone stays tightly shut until there is a wildfire. The fire clears the ground of other plants. At the same time, the fire's heat makes the cone open up. The seeds spill out on to the freshly burnt ground, where they have the best chance of growing.

Sturt's desert pea

Deserts are dry and bare of plants most of the time. It may not rain for several years. When it does rain, an amazing thing sometimes happens. The ground suddenly becomes covered with colourful flowers! Sturt's desert pea is one of the most colourful of these desert flowers.

The **stems** of Sturt's desert pea creep along the ground, but the flower stalks grow straight upwards.

After the rain

The flowers die soon after the rain stops. Their seeds fall to the ground and lie in the soil. Each seed has a hard coat that stops it from drying out. The seeds might lie in the soil for many years before the next rain falls. Then they quickly grow and produce flowers and more seeds.

The flowers of a Sturt's desert pea grow in little tufts around the stem. They make the flower look like a red paintbrush.

STURT'S DESERT PEA

HEIGHT:
UP TO 15 CENTIMETRES
(6 INCHES)

LIFESPAN:
OFTEN JUST A FEW MONTHS

HABITAT:
DESERT

THAT'S AMAZING!
THE COAT SURROUNDING A SEED IS SO TOUGH, GARDENERS HAVE TO RUB THE SEEDS WITH SANDPAPER TO WEAKEN THEM. IF THEY DO NOT, THE SEEDS WILL NOT GROW WHEN THEY PLANT THEM.

Papua New Guinea

Pacific Ocean

Indian Ocean

Australia

New Zealand

where Sturt's desert peas are found

Porcupine grass

Porcupine grass grows in the desert in the centre of Australia. This desert does get some rain, but the summer is so hot that the ground dries fast. Porcupine grass can survive here because it has long roots. They grow deep into the soil, searching for water. During the day, lizards and other animals hide in clumps of porcupine grass. They shelter here from the hot sunshine.

PORCUPINE GRASS

SIZE:
CLUMPS ARE UP TO 2 METRES (6 FEET) TALL AND 3 METRES (10 FEET) ACROSS

LIFESPAN:
25 YEARS OR MORE

HABITAT:
DESERTS AND DRY GRASSLANDS

THAT'S AMAZING!
ABORIGINES USED TO BURN PORCUPINE GRASS TO SEND SMOKE SIGNALS TO EACH OTHER ACROSS THE DESERT.

Papua New Guinea

Pacific Ocean

Indian Ocean

Australia

New Zealand

Tasmania

where porcupine grass is found

Porcupine grass grows in large, spiky clumps that look like porcupines.

Wildfires

Thunderstorms bring most of the desert's rain. The lightning causes wildfires that burn the porcupine grass. However, the shoots in the middle of the clumps are protected from the fire. They quickly grow again. The fire leaves behind patches of bare soil. Here, seeds take in rain from the storm and grow into new plants.

Apart from porcupine grass, very few plants grow in the Australian desert.

Mount Cook buttercup

Mount Cook buttercups grow high in the mountains. In winter, the ground is covered with snow. The leaves and flowers die, but an underground stem survives. In spring, the snow melts and the underground stem uses the melted water to grow new leaves.

Thirsty plant

Mount Cook buttercups grow beside mountain streams and in wet hollows. The flowers need plenty of water to grow tall and make seeds.

Mount Cook buttercups grow halfway up New Zealand's highest mountains.

In summer, patches of Mount Cook buttercups form carpets of tall white-and-yellow flowers.

Animal food

In some places Mount Cook buttercups have all been eaten by deer and other animals. They survive only on rocky cliffs out of reach of the animals.

MOUNT COOK BUTTERCUP

HEIGHT:
UP TO 1.5 METRES (5 FEET)

LIFESPAN:
SEVERAL YEARS

HABITAT:
HIGH MOUNTAINSIDES

THAT'S AMAZING!
MOUNT COOK BUTTERCUPS ARE THE LARGEST TYPE OF BUTTERCUP IN THE WORLD.

where Mount Cook buttercups are found

New Zealand

Pacific Ocean

Wollemi pine

Wollemi pines were growing 200 million years ago. Dinosaurs probably ate their leaves. Scientists thought they had all died out long ago. Then some living trees were discovered in a rocky **gorge** in a national park not far from Sydney. The trees are so rare that the place where they grow is kept secret.

WOLLEMI PINE

HEIGHT:
UP TO 40 METRES (130 FEET)

LIFESPAN:
400 YEARS

HABITAT:
ROCKY MOUNTAIN GORGES

THAT'S AMAZING!
SCIENTISTS WHO STUDY WOLLEMI PINES IN THE WILD ARE BLINDFOLDED AND LED TO THE SITE WHERE THEY GROW. THIS KEEPS THE PLACE A SECRET.

Papua New Guinea

Pacific Ocean

Indian Ocean

Australia

New Zealand

Tasmania

where Wollemi pines are found

Wollemi pines were found in this gorge in Wollemi National Park in 1994.

Long-living root

The trunks of Wollemi pines survive for about 400 years, but their roots can live much longer. When one trunk dies, a new trunk grows from the roots. The roots can survive for about 2,000 years.

Conifer trees

Pine trees are **conifers**. Conifer trees produce cones that hold the seeds. The leaves of pines and many other conifers are long needles. Conifer trees appeared on Earth before broad-leaved trees.

This Wollemi pine has been specially planted in a **botanical garden**.

Fibreball weed

Salty water kills most plants, but fibreball weed grows well in the sea. Fibreball weed is a seagrass. It can survive in the sea because the liquid inside the plant is even saltier than sea water! Seagrasses grow close together and form **meadows**, just as grass does on land.

Fibreball weed grows under the sea, but it is not a seaweed. It is a flowering plant.

FIBREBALL WEED

HEIGHT:
UP TO 80 CENTIMETRES
(30 INCHES)

LIFESPAN:
SEVERAL YEARS

HABITAT:
SHELTERED SEABEDS

THAT'S AMAZING!
THE LEAVES OF FIBREBALL WEED CAN GROW UP TO 3 CENTIMETRES (1 INCH) A DAY. IF HUMANS GREW THIS FAST, AN 8-WEEK-OLD BABY WOULD BE ABOUT THE HEIGHT YOU ARE NOW!

Papua New Guinea

Pacific Ocean

Indian Ocean

Australia

New Zealand

Tasmania

where fibreball weeds are found

Pollen strings

Seagrasses have flowers, but they do not rely on insects to take their pollen from one flower to another. Instead the flowers make strings of sticky pollen. The strings float in the sea until they wrap themselves around the flower of another plant. The plant gets its name "fibreball" because it has brown stringy fibres around the bottom of the leaves. These break off and roll around, twisting themselves into a ball.

Young lobsters spend the first three years of their life sheltering among fibreball weeds.

Plants in danger

Some plants are in danger of becoming **extinct** in the wild. This means that so few still grow there that they could disappear altogether. For example, Davies' waxflower grows wild only in three places along the George River in Tasmania. Here they grow close to meadows where cows could trample on them. Fences have been built around the waxflowers to protect them.

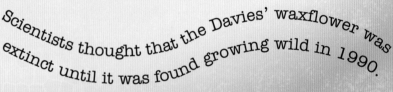

Scientists thought that the Davies' waxflower was extinct until it was found growing wild in 1990.

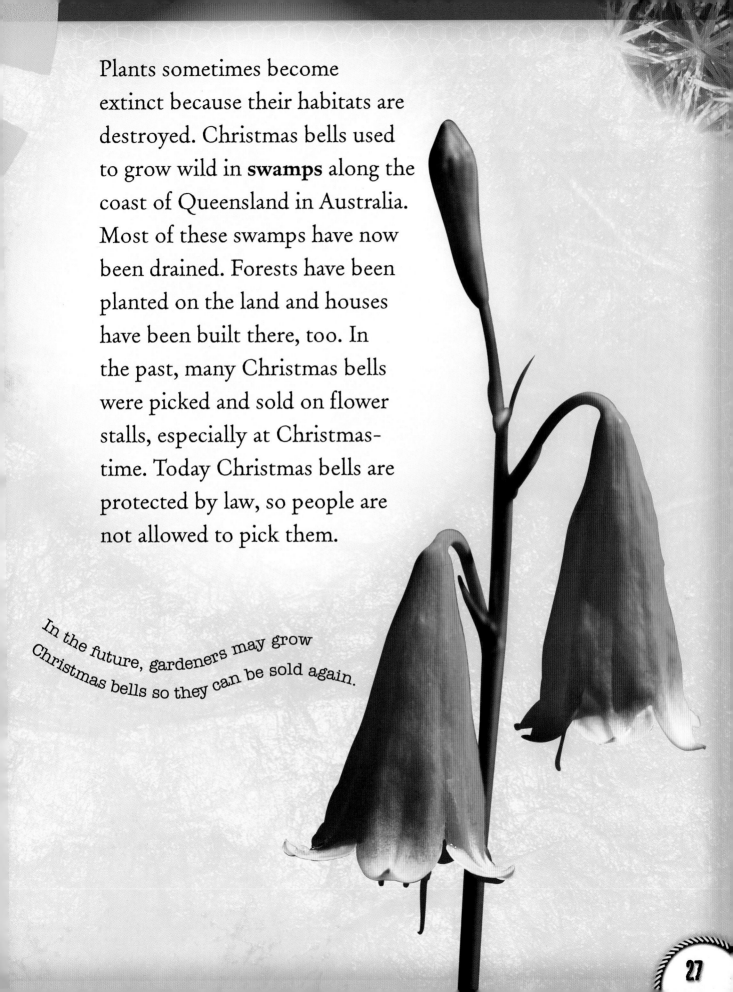

Plants sometimes become extinct because their habitats are destroyed. Christmas bells used to grow wild in **swamps** along the coast of Queensland in Australia. Most of these swamps have now been drained. Forests have been planted on the land and houses have been built there, too. In the past, many Christmas bells were picked and sold on flower stalls, especially at Christmas-time. Today Christmas bells are protected by law, so people are not allowed to pick them.

In the future, gardeners may grow Christmas bells so they can be sold again.

Plant facts and figures

There are millions of different kinds of plants growing all over the world. The place where a plant lives is called its habitat. Plants have special features, such as flowers, leaves, and stems. These features allow plants to survive in their habitats. Which plant do you think is the most amazing?

GUM TREE

HEIGHT:
2–100 METRES (6–330 FEET)

LIFESPAN:
UP TO 400 YEARS
(GIANT GUM)

HABITAT:
WOODLANDS

THAT'S AMAZING!
A KOALA EATS ABOUT 500 GRAMS (1 LB) OF GUM TREE LEAVES EVERY NIGHT. IF A PERSON ATE THAT MANY, THE GUM WOULD MAKE THEM VERY ILL.

STRANGLER FIG

HEIGHT:
UP TO 60 METRES (195 FEET)

LIFESPAN:
SEVERAL HUNDRED YEARS

HABITAT:
RAINFOREST

THAT'S AMAZING!
WHEN BIRDS AND SMALL ANIMALS EAT THE FRUIT OF STRANGLER FIGS, THE SEEDS PASS THROUGH THEIR BODIES. SOME DROP INTO SOIL HIGH IN THE TREES AND BEGIN TO GROW THERE.

MAIDEN VEIL TOADSTOOL

HEIGHT:
UP TO 20 CENTIMETRES (8 INCHES)

LIFESPAN:
THE TOADSTOOL LASTS ONLY A FEW DAYS

HABITAT:
RAINFOREST

THAT'S AMAZING!
MAIDEN VEIL TOADSTOOLS SMELL SO BAD, PEOPLE CANNOT BEAR THE SMELL EVEN 90 METRES (100 YARDS) AWAY.

MAMAKU

HEIGHT:
UP TO 20 METRES (65 FEET)

LIFESPAN:
50–100 YEARS

HABITAT:
OPEN WOODLAND

THAT'S AMAZING!
TREE-FERNS HAVE BEEN ON EARTH LONGER THAN MOST OTHER PLANTS. DINOSAURS USED TO ROAM THROUGH FORESTS OF TREE-FERNS.

BANKSIA

HEIGHT:
UP TO 30 METRES
(100 FEET)

LIFE SPAN:
PROBABLY
5–50 YEARS

HABITAT:
SCRUBLAND AND
FORESTS

THAT'S AMAZING!
MORE THAN A MILLION
FLOWER HEADS OF
BANKSIA ARE COLLECTED
AND SOLD IN FLOWER
SHOPS EACH YEAR.

STURT'S DESERT PEA

HEIGHT:
UP TO 15 CENTIMETRES
(6 INCHES)

LIFE SPAN:
OFTEN JUST A FEW
MONTHS

HABITAT:
DESERT

THAT'S AMAZING!
THE COAT SURROUNDING
A SEED IS SO TOUGH,
GARDENERS HAVE TO
RUB THE SEEDS WITH
SANDPAPER TO WEAKEN
THEM. IF THEY DO NOT,
THE SEEDS WILL NOT
GROW WHEN THEY
PLANT THEM.

PORCUPINE GRASS

SIZE:
CLUMPS ARE UP TO
2 METRES (6 FEET) TALL
AND 3 METRES
(10 FEET) ACROSS

LIFE SPAN:
25 YEARS OR MORE

HABITAT:
DESERTS AND DRY
GRASSLANDS

THAT'S AMAZING!
ABORIGINES USED TO
BURN PORCUPINE GRASS
TO SEND SMOKE SIGNALS
TO EACH OTHER ACROSS
THE DESERT.

MOUNT COOK BUTTERCUP

HEIGHT:
UP TO 1.5 METRES (5 FEET)

LIFE SPAN:
SEVERAL YEARS

HABITAT:
HIGH MOUNTAINSIDES

THAT'S AMAZING!
MOUNT COOK
BUTTERCUPS ARE THE
LARGEST TYPE OF
BUTTERCUP IN
THE WORLD.

WOLLEMI PINE

HEIGHT:
UP TO 40 METRES
(130 FEET)

LIFE SPAN:
400 YEARS

HABITAT:
ROCKY MOUNTAIN
GORGES

THAT'S AMAZING!
SCIENTISTS WHO STUDY
WOLLEMI PINES IN THE
WILD ARE BLINDFOLDED
AND LED TO THE SITE
WHERE THEY GROW.
THIS KEEPS THE PLACE
A SECRET.

FIBREBALL WEED

HEIGHT:
UP TO 80 CENTIMETRES
(30 INCHES)

LIFE SPAN:
SEVERAL YEARS

HABITAT:
SHELTERED SEABEDS

THAT'S AMAZING!
THE LEAVES OF FIBREBALL
WEED CAN GROW UP TO
3 CENTIMETRES (1 INCH)
A DAY. IF HUMANS GREW
THIS FAST, AN 8-WEEK-
OLD BABY WOULD BE
ABOUT THE HEIGHT YOU
ARE NOW!

Find out more

Books to read

Animals and Plants, Andrew Langley (Oxford University Press, 2002)

Plant Life Cycles, Anita Ganeri (Heinemann Library, 2006)

Plants and Planteaters (Secrets of the Rainforest), Michael Chinery (Crabtree Publishing Company, 2000)

Plants and the Environment, Jennifer Boothroyd (Lerner Publishing Group, 2007)

Plants that Eat Animals, Allan Fowler (Children's Press, 2001)

The Power of Plants, Claire Lewellyn (Oxford University Press, 2005)

The World's Largest Plants, Susan Blackaby (Picture Window Books, 2005)

Websites

www.australiaplants.com/au_plants_a-b-c.htm
Discover more about the plants of Australia.

www.kidsgeo.com/geography-for-kids/0153-biosphere.php
Learn more about weather, habitats, and how plants survive in them.

www.gardens.co.nz/natives.cfm
Lots of information and photographs about the native plants of New Zealand.

www.mbgnet.net/bioplants/adapt.html
Discover how plants adapt to different habitats, including deserts, grasslands, tropical rainforests, temperate forests, tundra, and water.

Glossary

Aborigines people who have lived in Australia since before the Europeans arrived

botanical garden garden where different kinds of plant are specially grown and studied

broad-leaved having flat, thin leaves

cone part of a conifer tree that carries the seeds

conifer tree that produces its seeds in cones

desert place that gets very little rain and has very few plants

extinct no longer in existence

flower head cluster of flowers on a stem

frond leaf of a fern

fungus (plural **fungi**) group of living things that feed on other living or dead things

gorge narrow valley with steep sides

grassland wide area covered in grass with few trees

habitat place where particular kinds of plant grow and where particular animals live

meadow grassy land, often near a river

nutrient part of food that is needed for health

pollen grains of yellow dust made by flowers

rainforest forest where it rains almost every day and where plants and trees grow close together

root part of a plant that takes in water and nutrients and anchors the plant in the soil

seed part of a plant or tree that can grow into a new plant or tree

spore seed of the type made by ferns, mosses, and fungi

stem part of a plant on which leaves or a flower grow

swamp very wet, soft land

tropical rainforest rainforest that grows near the Equator, where it is hot all year round

wildfire fire that starts by accident in the wild and is difficult to put out

Index